PRAISE FOR *SAVORY VS. SWEET*

"Shalean and Stephanie create recipes that are not only delicious, but absolutely beautiful to look at. This book has something for the whole family!"

—Cari Garcia, founder of FatgirlHedonist.com

"Steph and Shay have created the ultimate party in a book! The recipe ideas are fun, creative, and easy to follow. This book is truly an inspiration for any occasion, as there are creations for all skill sets and tastes. @soflofooodie has captured what cooking is about, FUN!"

—Ainsley Sheppard, Owner/Operator Cream Parlor, @Creamparlor

"Whether you're feeling sweet or salty, every single recipe in this book is lip-smackingly delicious, guaranteed to bring big smiles to your kitchen. This book is full of sensational treats that yield really impressive results for any home cook. 5 (rainbow-colored) stars!!!"

—Michael Silverstein, TV chef and bestselling author of *New Comfort Cooking*

"After numerous successful brand partnerships with @SoFloFooodie, I knew their cookbook would not disappoint. I am so excited to see their delicious recipes in one place and cannot wait to try some new desserts!"

—May Naish, influencer specialist

Savory
Vs. Sweet

Cover Design: Elina Diaz
Cover Photo/illustration: Shalean and Stephanie Ghitis
Layout & Design: Elina Diaz

For permission requests, please contact the publisher at:
Mango Publishing Group
2850 S Douglas Road, 4th Floor
Coral Gables, FL 33134 USA
info@mango.bz

For special orders, quantity sales, course adoptions and corporate sales, please email the publisher at sales@mango.bz. For trade and wholesale sales, please contact Ingram Publisher Services at customer.service@ingramcontent.com or +1.800.509.4887.

Savory Vs. Sweet: From Our Simple Two-Ingredient Recipes to Our Most Viral Unicorn Rainbow Cheesecake

Library of Congress Cataloging-in-Publication number: 2022940957
ISBN: (hardcover) 978-1-64250-991-5, (ebook) 978-1-64250-992-2
BISAC category code: CKB062000, COOKING / Courses & Dishes / Pastry

Printed in China

Savory
Vs. Sweet

From Our Simple Two-Ingredient Recipes
to our Most Viral Unicorn Rainbow Cheesecake

**Shalean Ghitis & Stephanie Ghitis
from SoFloFooodie**

CORAL GABLES

TABLE OF CONTENTS

1

Throwbacks   11

Some of the delicious nostalgic treats that we all know and love from the 1990s, but with a homemade twist.

2

Cheesecakes Galore   29

A chapter dedicated to a combination of baked and no-bake cheesecakes with a modern twist.

3

Savory Snacks   49

Savory recipes don't need to be complicated—simple and easy recipes do just the trick for those everyday cravings.

4

Cookies, Cakes, Brownies, and Bars 67

In this chapter, you'll find everything you need to satisfy your sweet tooth with simple but delicious dessert recipes.

6

Two-to-Seven-Ingredient Recipes 109

In a rush, but craving something tasty? Try out one of these easy recipes that require just a few simple ingredients you probably already have in your kitchen.

5

Breakfast and Brunch 87

Whether you're an early or late riser, this chapter is filled with a combination of sweet and savory breakfast and brunch items to start your day.

INTRODUCTION

Are you on Team Sweet, or Team Savory? We developed this mash-up cookbook to allow readers the ability to unleash their creativity and show off which side they're on. Whether you're into trendy savory cheese pulls or viral simple-ingredient desserts, this book has everything you need to explore the best of both worlds.

The recipes in this book were created so individuals of all skill levels and abilities could participate and have fun in the kitchen. We used easily accessible ingredients that many will already have in their kitchens, or will have the ability to obtain effortlessly. We want readers of all ages to use this cookbook to express themselves and their love for baking/cooking.

Whether you want to use the recipes included for a date night or game night bake-off, or want to wow guests at the next gathering, our hope is that you have fun in the process and make meaningful connections.

Be sure to use the hashtag #soflosavoryxsweet on social media when making a recipe from our book for a chance to be featured by us.

Thank you for all your support in helping this cookbook be a success!

Xo,

Shay
and Steph

1

THROWBACKS

This chapter is dedicated to those elementary school days when we would open our lunch boxes and find those delicious '90s snacks. This inspired us to make all types of snacks, including brownies, cookies, and cakes. This chapter will take you back to your nostalgic childhood days we all know and love!

RAINBOW CHIP BROWNIES

Makes 9 brownie squares.

Brownie Ingredients:
10 tbsp salted butter (melted)
1 cup (200 g/7 oz) granulated
    sugar
½ cup (100 g/3.5 oz)
    brown sugar
1 tsp vanilla
2 eggs
¾ cup (90 g/3 oz) sifted
    cocoa powder
⅔ cup (77 g/3 oz) cake flour
½ tbsp cornstarch
1 tbsp corn syrup

Frosting Ingredients:
1 ½ cups (240 g/9 oz)
    chocolate chips
½ cup (120 g/4 oz) heavy cream
Rainbow candy chips
    (found on Amazon)

Tip: Use a paper towel to clean the knife between slices for neat squares.

Directions:

1. Preheat the oven to 350ºF and line an 8x8" baking pan with parchment paper.

2. In a large bowl, combine the melted butter, granulated sugar, and brown sugar. Then mix in the eggs and vanilla.

3. Stir in the cocoa powder, flour, cornstarch, and corn syrup.

4. Pour the prepared batter into the prepared baking pan and bake for 25 minutes.

5. Allow to cool completely after removing from the oven.

6. In a microwave, melt together the chocolate chips and heavy cream in 15-second bursts until a chocolate ganache is formed.

7. Pour the ganache on top of the cooled brownies, along with the candy bits, and refrigerate for 1 hour (or until set).

CRÈME-FILLED SNACK CAKES

Makes 12 cakes.

Snack Cake Ingredients:

1 cup (130 g/4.6 oz)
   all-purpose flour
¾ cup (86 g/3 oz) cake flour
2 tsp baking powder
¼ tsp salt
1 cup (244 g/8.6 oz) whole milk
1¼ cup (200 g/7 oz)
   granulated sugar
2 tsp vanilla
2 eggs
1 egg yolk
2 egg whites
¼ tsp cream of tartar
¾ cup (170 g/6 oz) butter
   (room temperature)

Filling Ingredients:

4 oz (113 g) Cool Whip or
   homemade whipped cream
4 oz (113.2 g) marshmallow
   crème or fluff

Directions:

1. Preheat the oven to 325ºF.

2. In a small bowl, beat the egg whites and cream of tartar to stiff peaks. Set aside in the fridge.

3. In a medium bowl, combine the flour, baking powder, and salt, then set aside.

4. In a large bowl, cream together the butter and granulated sugar. Add your eggs, egg yolk, and vanilla. Beat for a few minutes until creamy (it's okay if there are lumps).

5. Add half the dry mixture to the wet egg mixture and combine. Then add the milk and remaining dry mixture and combine again.

6. Once fully combined, **fold** in half the whipped egg whites, then the other half. Once well folded in, pour into the baking pan cavities, filling each about ¾ full.

7. Bake for 18–20 minutes, or until a toothpick inserted into the center comes out clean. In a small bowl, combine the filling ingredients, then add to a piping bag.

8. Once the cakes are cool, poke three holes into the bottom of each. Fill each hole with the filling. Remove any excess.

Tip: Use a chopstick to easily poke the holes into the bottom of each cake.

CHOCOLATE 'n' CREME CUPCAKES

Makes 12 cupcakes.

Cupcake Ingredients:

1 cup (130 g/4.6 oz)
    all-purpose flour

½ cup (58 g/2 oz) cake flour

½ cup (60 g/2 oz) cocoa powder

¾ cup (150g/5.3 oz)
    granulated sugar

1 egg

½ cup (109 g/3.8 oz) vegetable oil

½ cup (122 g/4.3 oz) whole milk

½ cup (118 g/4 oz) hot water

½ tsp salt

1 tsp vanilla

1 tsp baking soda

**Marshmallow Filling
  Ingredients:**

½ cup (120 g/4 oz) heavy cream

½ cup (144 g/5 oz)
    marshmallow crème or fluff

Ganache Ingredients:

¼ cup (60 g/2 oz) heavy cream

½ cup (80 g/3 oz) chocolate chips

Icing Ingredients:

½ cup (60 g/2 oz) powdered sugar

1 tbsp heavy cream

Tip: To easily core the centers of your cupcakes, use the bottom of a large cake-decorating tip.

Directions:

1. Preheat the oven to 310ºF and line a cupcake pan with cupcake liners.

2. In a large mixing bowl, combine the milk, vegetable oil, egg, granulated sugar, vanilla, and hot water.

3. Sift in the two types of flour, salt, baking soda, and cocoa powder. Mix until smooth. Fill your cupcake liners about halfway.

4. Bake for 20 minutes, or until a toothpick inserted comes out clean. Allow to cool down.

5. Make the filling by whipping the heavy cream until stiff peaks form, then add the marshmallow crème and mix until combined.

6. Pour into a piping bag or Ziploc bag.

7. Core the centers of your cupcakes, leaving a small layer of cupcake at the bottom.

8. Fill the hole with the marshmallow filling and top with the removed cupcake piece.

9. Make your ganache by microwaving the heavy cream and chocolate chips in 15-second bursts.

10. Dip the cupcakes into the ganache and allow to dry (or pop in the freezer for 10 minutes).

11. Make your icing by combining the two ingredients, and decorate the tops of your cupcakes in "loops."

FUDGY SANDWICH COOKIES

Makes 8 sandwiches.

Sandwich Ingredients:
¾ cup (98 g/3.5 oz)
    all-purpose flour
¼ cup (33 g/1 oz) cake flour
½ cup (100 g/3.5 oz)
    granulated sugar
¼ cup (30 g/1 oz) cocoa powder
1 egg
1 tbsp vanilla
1 tbsp corn syrup
10 tbsp butter (softened)
1 tsp baking soda
Pinch of salt

Filling Ingredients:
8 tbsp softened butter
¼ tsp vanilla
3 tbsp cocoa powder
1¼ cups (150 g/6 oz)
    powdered sugar
Splash of warm water (optional)

**Chocolate Drizzle
    Ingredients:**
¼ cup (40 g/1.5 oz)
    chocolate chips
1 tsp oil (vegetable or coconut)

Tip: When piping your filling, less is more. It will expand when you add the other cookie on top.

Directions:

1. Preheat the oven to 350ºF and line a baking sheet with parchment paper.

2. In a medium bowl, combine both flours, cocoa powder, baking soda, and salt.

3. In a large bowl, using a hand mixer, beat the butter and granulated sugar on medium speed until light and fluffy, then add egg, corn syrup, and vanilla.

4. Pour the dry ingredients into the wet ingredients and continue to beat until well combined.

5. Use a cookie dough scooper to place 6 rounds at a time onto the baking sheet.

6. Bake for 9 minutes and allow to cool completely. Repeat with the remaining dough.

7. Combine filling ingredients (minus the warm water) in a medium bowl using a hand mixer. Once combined, if the filling is too thick or clumpy, add one splash of the warm water at a time to thin it out.

8. Pipe a thin layer of filling onto the inside of one cookie, then top with another cookie to form a sandwich.

9. In a small bowl, combine the chocolate chips and oil, then microwave in 15-second bursts until smooth and silky.

10. Pour into a piping or Ziploc bag and drizzle on top of one side of the sandwiches.

CHOCOLATE CRISPY PATTIES

Makes 10 cookies.

Ingredients:

½ cup (80 g/3 oz) chocolate chips

½ cup (145 g/10 oz)
    dulce de leche

2 tbsp butter

2½ cups (125 g/4.5 oz)
    mini marshmallows

2 cups (84 g/2 oz) Rice Krispies
    (or similar) cereal

Tip: Use cooking spray on your hands when rolling the mixture into balls to prevent sticking.

Directions:

1. Melt the chocolate chips and butter in the microwave in 15-second bursts until smooth and silky.

2. Add the dulce de leche and marshmallows to the chocolate mixture, then microwave for 1 minute.

3. Stir in the cereal.

4. Once warm to the touch, scoop ¼-cup rounds, roll each into a ball, and place on parchment paper.

5. Flatten into disk shapes.

6. Allow to cool and set completely.

PEANUT BUTTER COOKIE SANDWICHES

Makes 24 sandwich cookies.

Cookie Ingredients:

1½ cups (195 g/7 oz)
  all-purpose flour
8 tbsp softened butter
1 cup (200 g/7 oz)
  packed brown sugar
1 egg
1 tsp baking soda
½ tsp salt
1 tsp vanilla extract
¾ cup (180 g/6.5 oz)
  creamy peanut butter
Granulated sugar for rolling

Filling Ingredients:

1½ cups (180 g/6.5 oz)
  powder sugar
½ cup (120 g/4 oz) creamy
  peanut butter
2 tbsp softened butter
2 tbsp milk
½ tsp vanilla extract

Tip: If you don't have peanut butter, you can just blend peanuts and a pinch of salt in a blender until smooth and creamy. This recipe was made using homemade peanut butter!

Directions:

1. Preheat oven to 350ºF.

2. In a large bowl, using a hand mixer, combine butter and brown sugar until well mixed and fluffy.

3. Add the egg and vanilla and mix again.

4. Add the flour, baking soda, salt, and peanut butter, then beat on medium speed until fully combined.

5. Cover the dough with plastic wrap and refrigerate for about 30 minutes.

6. Roll the dough into small (1-inch) rounds, then roll into granulated sugar.

7. Once coated in sugar, form the rounds into small logs about 2 inches long and half an inch thick.

8. Place the logs on a baking sheet and press down slightly to smooth out.

9. Use a fork to create crisscross lines and holes, and pinch the center of each log to resemble a peanut. You may need to use your hands to help shape each into a peanut shape.

10. Bake for 5 minutes, then allow the cookies to finish cooling on the baking sheet for 5 minutes more before transferring.

11. While the cookies are baking, mix the filling ingredients together, using a hand mixer to create a smooth peanut butter filling.

12. Once the cookies are cool, spread a small amount of the filling onto one of the cookies and add another cookie to create a "sandwich."

OATMEAL *'n'* CRÈME PATTIES

Makes 18 sandwiches.

Sandwich Ingredients:

2 cups (160 g/6 oz) quick oats

¾ cup (170 g/6 oz) butter
(room temperature)

1 cup (200 g/7 oz)
granulated sugar

½ cup (100 g/3.5 oz)
brown sugar

2 eggs

2 tbsp maple syrup

2 tsp baking soda

1½ tsp salt

1 tsp baking powder

1½ tsp cinnamon

Filling Ingredients:

8 tbsp softened butter

1 cup (120 g/4.3 oz)
powdered sugar

7 oz (198 g) jar marshmallow
crème or fluff

1–2 tbsp heavy cream

Tip: Allowing the cookies to cool before adding the filling will ensure the filling doesn't melt.

Directions:

1. Preheat oven to 350ºF and line a baking sheet with parchment paper.

2. In a large bowl, using a hand mixer, combine butter, granulated and brown sugars, and maple syrup.

3. Add the eggs and mix. Then add the cinnamon, baking powder, baking soda, and salt. Mix again.

4. Fold in the flour and then the oats.

5. Use a cookie scoop to form rounds of dough, and place them on the baking sheet about 3 inches apart.

6. Bake for 10–12 minutes until golden. Allow the cookies to cool while you prepare the filling.

7. In a medium bowl, combine the filling ingredients, then place the filling in a piping bag.

8. Place about 2 tbsp of filling on the centers of half of the cookies. Use the other half of the cookies to top each of the cookies with the filling to form the sandwiches.

9. Push down on each sandwich to encourage the filling to spread to the edges of the sandwiches.

10. Allow the cookies to set.

CONFETTI CAKE DIP

Serves about 10.

Ingredients:

1 (432 g/15 oz) box
  Funfetti cake mix
8 oz (226 g) Cool Whip (thawed)
  or homemade whipped cream
2 (3¼-oz) vanilla pudding cups
4 tbsp rainbow sprinkles

Tip: You can also make a chocolate version using chocolate cake mix and chocolate pudding.

Directions:

1. In a large bowl, add the cake mix and microwave for 2 minutes, stirring halfway through. Ensure the temperature has reached 165°F (this kills the bacteria in the flour). Allow to cool for at least 10 minutes.

2. Add the thawed Cool Whip and combine.

3. Add the 2 vanilla pudding cups and mix again to combine.

4. Fold in the rainbow sprinkles.

5. Add to a serving dish.

6. Serve with your choice of dippers.

2
CHEESECAKES GALORE

Once our Unicorn Rainbow Cheesecake went viral in 2019, we decided to make different variations of cheesecakes for the everyday cheesecake lover. In this chapter you will find a combination of no-bake and baked cheesecakes that are sure to satisfy your cravings and wow your guests!

UNICORN RAINBOW CHEESECAKE (NO-BAKE)

Serves 8–10.

Crust Ingredients:

4 tbsp butter

10 oz (283 g) bag mini
marshmallows

6 cups (180 g/6 oz)
Rice Krispies (or similar) cereal

Cheesecake Ingredients:

20 oz (562.5 g) cream cheese
(softened)

½ cup (123 g/4.3 oz) sour cream
(room temperature)

2 cups (240 g/8.6 oz)
powdered sugar

2 cups (488 g/17 oz) cold
heavy whipping cream

1 tbsp vanilla extract

2½ cups (400 g/15 oz)
white chocolate

Pink, orange, yellow, green, blue,
and purple food coloring

Sprinkles to decorate

9-inch springform pan

Tip: If you prefer
a more traditional
crust, feel free to use
that instead of the
cereal crust.

Directions:

1. Completely melt the butter in a large saucepan over medium heat.

2. Add the marshmallows and stir until creamy.

3. Add the 6 cups of cereal and stir until fully mixed. Remove from heat immediately.

4. Transfer the cereal mixture to the springform pan. To do this, grease the inside of the pan generously to prevent sticking. Also, grease your hands slightly to easily transfer the cereal mixture to the pan (we use Pam baking spray). Use all of the cereal mixture to fill the bottom of the pan, and go up the sides too. We also used a measuring cup to easily mold the mixture into the pan. Remove any excess mixture at the top.

5. Put the crust into the fridge to set while you prepare the filling.

6. Using a hand or stand mixer, beat the whipping cream and 1 cup of powdered sugar until stiff peaks form. Be patient—this step can take a few minutes. Set aside.

7. In a separate large bowl, using a hand or stand mixer on medium speed, combine the cream cheese and the remaining powdered sugar until soft. Then mix in the sour cream and vanilla.

8. Heat the white chocolate in a double boiler until smooth and creamy, and allow to cool to room temperature while stirring occasionally. Cooling ensures the white chocolate doesn't harden when added to the cream cheese mixture.

9. Once cooled, start the mixer at low speed and add the room-temperature white chocolate slowly into the cream cheese mixture. Fold the whipping cream mixture into the cream cheese mixture using a spatula (be careful not to over-mix).

10. Separate the mixture into 6 small-size mixing bowls, and add a different color of food coloring to each bowl. The less food coloring, the lighter; the more food coloring, the darker/brighter. This choice is based on your preference.

11. Remove the crust from the fridge and pour the purple-colored mixture into the bottom of the crust, then freeze for 20–30 minutes.

12. Repeat this process with each color, making sure to freeze each layer for 20–30 minutes.

13. Decorate to your desire and place in the fridge to set for 6 hours (or overnight).

RED VELVET CHEESECAKE

Serves 8–10.

Crust Ingredients:

35 Oreos or chocolate crème
    cookies (finely crushed)
7 tbsp melted butter

Cheesecake Ingredients:

32 oz (900 g) cream cheese
    (softened)
1 cup (240g/8.6 oz) sour cream
    (room temperature)
1½ tbsp vanilla
1⅓ cups (266g/9 oz) granulated
    sugar
4 eggs (room temperature)
¼ cup (30g/1 oz) cocoa powder
Red food coloring (we used 1 oz)

Tip: Sometimes springform pans leak, which may ruin the texture of a cheesecake. To avoid this, you can wrap the bottom and edges of your pan with a few layers of aluminum foil. Amazon also sells a springform pan protector.

Directions:

1. Make your crust by combining finely crushed cookies (using a food processor is the best route) and melted butter, then spread the mixture into the bottom of a greased 9-inch springform pan.

2. Bake on 350ºF for 10 minutes, then set aside to cool.

3. In a large bowl, beat the cream cheese until creamy, then add sugar, cocoa powder, vanilla, sour cream, and eggs until fully combined.

4. Add your red food coloring until desired color is reached, and pour the batter into the cake pan with the crust.

5. Next, grab a larger pan (big enough for the 9-inch springform pan to fit in comfortably) and place a couple of paper towels on the bottom of it. Place the springform pan inside the larger pan with the paper towels, and fill the larger pan with boiling water to haltway up the side of the springform pan with the batter. Be careful not to get any water into the pan with the batter. This is a bain-marie, a very important step to help the cake bake evenly.

6. Bake the cheesecake at 300ºF for 1 hour and 20 minutes. Turn the oven off and leave the cheesecake in the oven for another 30 minutes with the door closed. Then open the door and leave in for an additional 15 minutes.

7. Remove the cheesecake from the oven and continue to cool to room temperature.

8. Cover with plastic wrap and refrigerate for 6 hours, or overnight.

9. Remove the sides of the springform pan and decorate to your desire.

CONFETTI CAKE CHEESECAKE

Serves 8–10.

Crust Ingredients:

35 Golden Oreos (or vanilla
   sandwich cookies)
5 tbsp melted butter
3 tbsp sprinkles

Filling Ingredients:

24 oz (675 g) cream cheese
   (softened)
¼ cup (50g/1.8 oz)
   granulated sugar
1 cup Funfetti cake mix
   (heat-treated, see below)
½ cup (80g/3 oz) white chocolate
   (melted & cooled)
1½ tsp vanilla cup (5 tbsp) sprinkles
1 cup (83 g/1.9 oz) Cool Whip or
   homemade whipped cream
5 crushed Golden Oreos (or vanilla
   sandwich cookies) (without the
   icing center)

Tip: Feel free to play
around with cake
mix flavors, such as
strawberry, for added
flavor to your confetti
cheesecake.

Directions:

1. Finely crush the vanilla sandwich cookies until the material resembles sand, then pour into a large bowl.

2. Add the melted butter and sprinkles to the crushed cookies. Mix to combine.

3. Pour the mixture into a greased 9-inch springform pan and place in the fridge to set while you make the filling.

4. Place the cake mix in the microwave for 2 minutes, or until it reaches 165°F (this kills any bacteria).

5. In a large bowl, using a hand mixer, cream together the cream cheese, sugar, and vanilla until smooth.

6. Beat in the heat-treated cake mix and cooled white chocolate.

7. Fold in the Cool Whip or whipped cream and sprinkles.

8. Pour the batter into the prepared pan and top with crushed cookies.

9. Refrigerate for 4–6 hours to completely set.

10. Top with additional dollops of Cool Whip or whipped cream and sprinkles.

MINI PUMPKIN CHEESECAKE CUPS

Makes 12 cups.

Crust Ingredients:

1 ½ cups (150 g)
    crushed graham cracker
6 tbsp melted butter

Filling Ingredients:

12 oz (338 g) cream cheese
    (softened)
½ cup (100 g/3.5 oz)
    granulated sugar
1 ½ tsp vanilla cup
⅓ cup (75 g/3 oz) pumpkin purée
1 tbsp pumpkin pie spice
2 eggs (room temperature)

**Pumpkin Whipped Cream
    Ingredients:**

½ cup (120 g/4 oz)
    heavy whipping cream
¼ cup (62 g/2.2 oz)
    pumpkin purée
2 tsp pumpkin pie spice
1 tbsp powdered sugar
Sprinkles for topping (optional)
Extra crushed graham cracker for
    topping (optional)

Directions:

1. Preheat the oven to 350ºF and line a cupcake pan with cupcake liners.

2. Finely crush the graham cracker until it resembles sand, and pour into a bowl.

3. Add the melted butter to the crushed graham crackers and mix to combine.

4. Put two large spoons of the mixture into the cupcake liners.

5. Bake for 5 minutes, then set aside.

6. Using a hand mixer, cream together the cream cheese, sugar, and vanilla until smooth.

7. Beat in the pumpkin purée and pumpkin pie spice.

8. Add the eggs and beat into the mixture until combined.

9. Pour two large spoonfuls of batter into each cupcake liner.

10. Bake for 14 minutes and allow to come to room temperature.

11. Place in the fridge for 2–3 hours to set.

12. To make the whipped cream, beat the whipped cream ingredients until thick.

13. Pipe each cheesecake with the pumpkin whipped cream, then top with sprinkles and extra crushed graham crackers if desired.

Tip: To quickly soften cream cheese, run the pack under warm water, or let it sit in a warm water bath for 5–10 minutes.

KEY LIME CHEESECAKE

Serves 8–10.

Crust Ingredients:

1½ cups (150 g)
   crushed graham cracker
6 tbsp melted butter

Filling Ingredients:

32 oz (900 g) cream cheese
   (softened)
1 cup (120g/4.3 oz)
   powdered sugar
1 cup (83 g/2.9 oz) homemade
   whipped cream or Cool Whip
6 key limes, or 6 tbsp key lime juice
Zest from 6 key limes

Tip: To make
homemade whipped
cream, simply beat
1 cup cold heavy
whipping cream to
stiff peaks.

Directions:

1. Finely crush the graham cracker until it resembles sand, then place in a large bowl.

2. Add the melted butter and mix to combine.

3. Pour the mixture into a greased 9-inch springform pan and refrigerate for 20 minutes.

4. Using a hand mixer, cream together the cream cheese and powdered sugar until smooth.

5. Add the key lime juice and half the zest and mix to fully combine.

6. Fold in the homemade whipped cream or Cool Whip.

7. Pour the mixture into the prepared springform pan.

8. Top with the remaining zest and refrigerate for 4–6 hours.

9. Top with extra dollops of whipped cream and sliced key limes if desired.

S'MORES CHEESECAKE BARS

**Makes 6 large bars,
or 9 squares.**

Crust Ingredients:
1 ½ cups (150 g) crushed
graham cracker
6 tbsp melted butter

Filling Ingredients:
24 oz (675 g) cream cheese
(softened)
½ cup (60g/2oz) powdered sugar
2 cups (100g/4 oz) mini
marshmallows or 1 cup
marshmallow crème/fluff

Ganache Ingredients:
1 ½ cups (240g/9 oz)
chocolate chips
½ cup (120g/4 oz) heavy cream

Topping Ingredients:
2 cups (110 g/3.8 oz)
mini marshmallows

Tip: When deciding what size pan to use, think about how thick or thin you want your end product.

Directions:

1. Finely crush the graham cracker until it resembles sand, then place in a large bowl.

2. Add the melted butter and mix to combine.

3. Pour the mixture into a greased 8x8" or 9x9" pan and refrigerate for 20 minutes.

4. Using a hand mixer, cream together the cream cheese and powdered sugar until smooth.

5. If using mini marshmallows instead of crème/fluff, microwave for about 30–45 seconds until melted.

6. Fold the melted marshmallow or crème/fluff into the mixture.

7. Pour the mixture into the prepared pan and refrigerate for 5 hours.

8. In a medium bowl, microwave the ganache ingredients for about a minute and mix to fully combine.

9. Pour on top of the cheesecake and freeze for 20 minutes.

10. Add the remaining mini marshmallows to the top, and either broil on 500ºF for a few minutes (watching carefully not to burn) or use a hand torch.

11. Continue to refrigerate, or serve as is.

STRAWBERRY CHEESECAKE CRUMB BARS

Makes 9 squares.

Dough Ingredients:

1½ cups (195 g/7 oz)
   all-purpose flour

½ cup (100 g/3.5oz)
   granulated sugar

1 beaten egg

2 tsp vanilla

½ tsp baking powder

½ tsp salt

½ cup (113g/4 oz) butter
   (cold and cubed)

Filling Ingredients:

2½ cups (415 g/12.5oz)
   chopped strawberries

½ cup (100 g/3.5oz)
   granulated sugar

2 tbsp brown sugar

1 tbsp cornstarch

4 oz (112.5 g) cream cheese
   (softened)

Directions:

1. Preheat the oven to 375°F.

2. In a large bowl, combine flour, sugar, salt, and baking powder, then add your butter.

3. Using a masher or fork, combine the mixture until crumbly. You may need to use your hands to mix it. Then add in your beaten egg and vanilla.

4. Mix until well combined and crumbly again.

5. Pour half the mixture into an 8x8" pan lined with parchment paper, pressing down.

6. In a medium bowl, combine all the filling ingredients until well mixed.

7. Pour on top of the crumb mixture in the pan, then add the remaining crumb dough on top. It's okay if there is filling showing.

8. Bake for 45–50 minutes, then allow to cool completely before slicing.

Tip: You can also use this filling recipe as a breakfast spread.

COOKIES 'n' CREAM CHEESECAKE DIP

Serves about 10.

Dip Ingredients:

1 cup (120 g/4 oz) powdered sugar

8 oz (226 g) Cool Whip or homemade whipped cream

10 oz (254 g) cream cheese (softened)

18–20 Oreos or chocolate crème cookies

Tip: Separating the crème from the cookies allows you to crush the cookies into small pieces without creating a mushy mess.

Directions:

1. Start by separating the crème filling from the cookies and placing in separate bowls.

2. Crush your cookies into small pieces (you don't want them completely crushed; you want small pieces), then set aside.

3. In a large mixing bowl, use a hand mixer to combine powdered sugar, cream cheese, and the crème filling until smooth.

4. Add the crushed cookies (leaving just a small amount to garnish) and fold in the Cool Whip or homemade whipped cream.

5. Place in a serving bowl and garnish with any remaining cookie crumbs.

6. Serve with your favorite dippers!

3

SAVORY SNACKS

Savory snacks and treats don't have to be complicated. Here you will find some of our favorite go-to savory recipes using everyday ingredients commonly found in most households, including our most viral savory dishes. From cheese pulls to flavorful seasonings, this chapter is sure to entice your taste buds!

CHIP-CRUSTED MAC ‘n’ CHEESE DONUT

Makes 6–8 large donuts.

Donut Ingredients:

2½ cups (250 g) uncooked
   elbow macaroni

4 tbsp butter

2 tbsp all-purpose flour

1 cup (244 g/8.6 oz) whole milk

16 oz (453 g) shredded cheese
   (we used cheddar and gouda)

1 tbsp garlic powder

1 tsp salt

1 tsp black pepper

Topping Ingredients:

3 eggs

1 cup (130 g/4.6 oz)
   all-purpose flour

8.5 oz (240.9 g) bag Cheetos
   or other chips of choice (crushed
   to powder)

Tip: Try this using any
of your favorite chips.

Directions:

1. Cook your pasta as instructed on the package and set aside.

2. Melt the butter over medium heat and add the flour. Whisk for one minute (no longer).

3. Add the milk and whisk until you see the cream thicken.

4. Add half the cheese, mix, and add the other half of the cheese.

5. The sauce should thicken as it cooks. When you see it thicken, add the cooked pasta and combine using a spatula.

6. Add the garlic powder and salt, then refrigerate for at least an hour.

7. Remove from the fridge and place a large scoop on a cutting board. Begin to form it into a donut shape using your hands. Cover using plastic wrap and freeze for 15–20 minutes.

8. Remove from the freezer and use something to form a hole in the center like a donut (we used a large icing tip).

9. Combine beaten eggs in one bowl, flour in another bowl, and chip crumbs in a third bowl.

10. Dip the mac and cheese donut into the egg, then the flour, then the egg again, and then the chip crumbs. Be sure to fully coat it in the crumbs.

11. Using a deep fryer on 350ºF (or a large pot with enough oil to fully submerge the donut), drop each donut into the hot oil until crispy and golden (around 4–5 minutes, flipping halfway). Do not let it burn. Fry the donuts one at a time.

12. When each is done, remove from the oil and pat dry with a paper towel.

PIZZA MONKEY BREAD

**Makes one 9–10-inch
Bundt panful.**

Ingredients:

2 (16 oz) cans refrigerated
    biscuit dough
2 tbsp olive oil
1 tbsp garlic powder
1 ½ tsp Italian seasoning
16 oz shredded mozzarella cheese
1 ½ cups (408 g/14 oz) pizza or
    marinara sauce
Pepperoni (optional)

Tip: Use this recipe as
a base, but switch up
the ingredients to make
a garlic and cheese
monkey bread.

Directions:

1. Preheat the oven to 350ºF. Cut each biscuit into quarters and place them in a large bowl.

2. Add the olive oil, Italian seasoning, garlic powder, and a third of the cheese.

3. Add some of the mixture to a greased 9- or 10-inch Bundt pan to cover the bottom of the pan.

4. Add half of the sauce, another third of the cheese, and half of the pepperoni (if using).

5. Cover with the remaining biscuit mix and repeat with the remaining sauce, cheese, and pepperoni.

6. Bake for 40–45 minutes, or until cooked through.

BUFFALO CHICKEN SLIDERS

Makes 9–12 sliders.

Ingredients:

1 package (9 or 12) Hawaiian rolls

1 cup (202 g/8.4 oz) buffalo sauce

6 tbsp melted butter

8 oz (226 g) shredded cheddar cheese

2½ cups (296 g/10.5 oz) shredded chicken

1 tbsp minced garlic

½ tsp Italian seasoning

Pinch of salt and pepper

Tip: Use a serrated knife when slicing bread of any kind to smoothly slide through.

Directions:

1. Preheat the oven to 350ºF.

2. Combine 3 tbsp of the melted butter with the buffalo sauce in a large bowl.

3. Add the shredded chicken to the bowl and fully coat in the sauce.

4. Cut the Hawaiian rolls in half, keeping the bottom and the top halves together, and place the bottom halves into either a greased 9x9" pan (for 9 rolls) or a greased 9x13" pan (for 12 rolls).

5. Spread half of the cheese onto the rolls.

6. Add the buffalo chicken mixture on top of the cheese.

7. Sprinkle the remaining cheese on top.

8. Place the roll tops directly over the cheese layer to form a large sandwich.

9. Bake for 15 minutes.

10. Combine the remaining 3 tbsp of melted butter with minced garlic, Italian seasoning, and a pinch of salt and pepper. Brush the mixture over the top of the sliders.

EASY ROUND LASAGNA

Serves 6.

Ingredients:

1 package (340 g/12 oz)
    oven-ready lasagna noodles

48 oz (1360 g) marinara or
    pasta sauce

1 pound ground beef

2 tbsp minced garlic

2 tbsp Italian seasoning

2 tsp onion powder

2 tbsp parsley

Pinch of salt and pepper

15 oz (425 g) ricotta cheese

16 oz shredded mozzarella cheese

½ cup (49 g/1.7 oz) grated
    parmesan cheese

1 tbsp olive oil

Tip: You can use this recipe in a 9x13" baking dish for a more traditional look.

Directions:

1. Bring a large pot of water to boil and place one package of lasagna noodles into the water, allowing them to cook for just a few minutes. We like to do this just to make them easier to shape in the round pan. Set aside.

2. In a small bowl, combine ricotta, Parmesan, half the mozzarella, parsley, and salt/pepper, then set aside.

3. Preheat the oven to 350ºF.

4. In a skillet, add your olive oil, minced garlic, and salt/pepper. Then add in your ground beef, Italian seasoning, and onion powder and cook until browned. Drain.

5. Add in your marinara or pasta sauce of choice and allow to simmer for about 10 minutes.

6. To a 9-inch springform pan, add a small amount of the meat sauce to the bottom, then begin layering: noodles, ricotta cheese mixture, meat sauce, then a nice coat of mozzarella cheese. Repeat. We did about 3–4 layers for the whole pan.

7. Cover with aluminum foil and bake for 25 minutes. Remove the foil and continue to bake another 15 minutes. Turn the oven to broil to brown the top for just a few minutes, watching carefully not to burn.

8. Remove from the oven and allow to sit for 10 minutes before removing the side of the springform pan.

SPICY RIGATONI PASTA

Ingredients:

1 16 oz (454 g) box rigatoni pasta

4 tbsp butter

¼ cup olive oil

1 tbsp minced (or fresh) garlic

6 oz (170 g) can tomato paste

1 ¼ cup (305 g/10.8 oz) heavy cream

2 tbsp cream cheese (softened)

¾ cup (73 g/2.5 oz) shredded parmesan cheese

2 tsp red pepper flakes

Salt and pepper

Parsley flakes

1 cup (236 g/8 oz) reserved pasta water

Tip: I add a little of the reserved pasta water into the leftover container so when I reheat it, it's nice and creamy.

Directions:

1. Cook your pasta according to the package instructions and set aside, along with 1 cup reserved pasta water.

2. In a saucepan over medium heat, add the olive oil and garlic, then add your tomato paste. Cook down for a couple of minutes.

3. Add the heavy cream, salt and pepper to taste, and red pepper flakes. Simmer for about 2 minutes.

4. Add the cream cheese, butter, and Parmesan cheese. Then add ¾ cup of the reserved pasta water. Mix until smooth and creamy.

5. Toss the cooked pasta into the sauce. You can either add the remaining pasta water, discard it, or save it for use with any leftovers (see tip below).

6. Serve and top with the parsley flakes.

SPINACH *and* ARTICHOKE DIP *in a* BREAD BOWL

Serves 10–12.

Ingredients:

8 oz cream cheese (softened)

8 tbsp butter

16 oz (453 g) sour cream

1 tbsp garlic

10 oz frozen spinach

8 oz mozzarella cheese

½ cup (48.5 g/1.7 oz)
  Parmesan cheese

14 oz (396 g) can of artichokes
  (chopped)

1 large round loaf of bread of
  choice (unsliced)

Tip: Try it cold too!

Directions:

1. Cut a circle along the top of the bread loaf about 2 inches into the loaf and remove the circle top.

2. Begin to hollow the bread from the inside of the loaf to create a bowl shape.

3. Over medium heat, add the garlic, butter, and cream cheese. Heat together until almost fully melted.

4. Add in the sour cream and combine.

5. Add the frozen spinach and allow to cook until fully melted down.

6. Cut up the canned artichoke (how fine depends on how big you would like the chunks), then add into the mixture.

7. Add both types of cheese and, once fully melted, remove from heat.

8. Pour the warm dip into the bread bowl and serve.

RAINBOW GRILLED CHEESE

Makes 2 sandwiches.

Ingredients:

8 oz shredded mozzarella cheese

2 tbsp softened butter

4 slices of thick brioche bread

Pink, orange, yellow, green, blue,
  and pink food coloring

Tip: Use whole milk
mozzarella for the
best cheese pulls.

Directions:

1. Separate the cheese equally into 6 bowls. Color each bowl of cheese with a different color of food coloring.

2. Butter all 4 slices of bread, then flip 2 of the slices over, butter side down.

3. Add rows of each colored cheese on the 2 slices, then top with the remaining slices of bread (this time butter side up).

4. Add to a skillet and cook each side on medium high until golden and cheese is melted through.

5. Cut the sandwiches perpendicular to the rainbow rows on each side (only cutting through the bread, not all the way through the sandwich, so you can get the cheese pull).

CHICKEN PARM SANDWICHES

Makes 2 sandwiches.

Ingredients:

Two 6-inch sub rolls of choice

2 eggs (whisked)

2 chicken cutlets (seasoned)

1 cup (119 g/4.2 oz)
    bread crumbs

4–6 slices of mozzarella cheese

½ cup (136 g/4.8 oz)
    marinara sauce

Fresh basil

Sprinkle of shredded Parmesan

Tip: If you want a panini but don't have a panini maker, add a heavy piece of cookware on top of your sandwich during step 5 to flatten.

Directions:

1. Turn your grill, oven, or panini maker to 350ºF.

2. Coat the seasoned chicken in the whisked egg, then completely coat in bread crumbs.

3. Fry the chicken cutlets in oil until golden and internal temperature reaches 165ºF.

4. Assemble the sandwiches by adding a layer of marinara, the cooked cutlet, more marinara, sliced cheese, basil, and Parmesan.

5. Place the sandwich on the grill or panini maker, or in the oven. Allow to cook for a few minutes until the cheese is melted.

4

COOKIES, CAKES, BROWNIES, *and* BARS

Whether you're looking for a unique cookie recipe or a traditional fudge brownie, this chapter is packed with indulgent and flavorful dessert recipes to satisfy your sweet tooth. Here is where you can find a sweet recipe for the everyday cravings, or even something to serve at your next get-together!

COSMIC COOKIES

Makes 8–10 cookies.

Cookie Ingredients:

1 cup (130 g/4.6 oz)
   all-purpose flour

⅓ cup (38 g/1.5 oz) cake flour

½ cup (60 g/2.1 oz) cocoa powder

¾ cup (150 g/5.3) granulated sugar

1 egg

3 tbsp vegetable oil

2 tsp vanilla

1 tsp baking powder

½ cup (113 g/4 oz) butter (melted)

Pinch of salt

½ cup (80 g/3 oz) chocolate chips

Ganache Ingredients:

1 cup (160 g/6 oz) chocolate chips

¼ cup (60 g/2 oz) heavy cream

Rainbow baking chips

Tip: Find the rainbow baking chips on Amazon.

Directions:

1. Preheat the oven to 350ºF.

2. In a large bowl, combine sugar, egg, vegetable oil, butter, and vanilla.

3. Once combined, add in your flours, salt, baking powder, cocoa powder, and chocolate chips. Mix well until combined.

4. Line a baking tray with parchment paper and add your cookie scoops onto the tray. You can make them as big or little as you wish.

5. Push down on the scoops as much or as little as you want, depending on how thick you want them. Bake for 12 minutes.

6. Remove the cookies from the oven and allow to cool for 5 minutes on the tray, then move them off the tray and allow to cool for another 5 minutes.

7. Combine the chocolate chips and heavy cream and microwave in 15-second bursts until melted.

8. Add the ganache to the top of each cookie, along with the rainbow baking chips.

ONE-BOWL PERFECT BROWNIES

Makes 9 squares.

Brownie Ingredients:

1 ¼ cups (163 g/5.8 oz) all-purpose flour

⅓ cup (39 g/4.2 oz) cocoa powder

1 cup (227 g/8 oz) unsalted butter

1 cup (200 g/7 oz) granulated sugar

¾ cup (150 g/5.3 oz) brown sugar

1 tbsp vanilla

1 cup (160 g/6 oz) chocolate chips

½ cup (80 g/3 oz) chopped chocolate

3 eggs

1 tsp salt

Tip: Using chopped chocolate ensures rich and ultra-chocolatey brownies.

Directions:

1. Preheat the oven to 350ºF.

2. In a large bowl, combine butter and chocolate chips.

3. Microwave in 15-second bursts (for about 1 ½ minutes), and whisk together until silky smooth.

4. Add in your sugars, salt, vanilla, and eggs, then mix well.

5. Sift in the flour and cocoa powder, then fold until completely incorporated.

6. Add in chopped chocolate and pour the mixture into an 8x8" pan lined with parchment paper.

7. Bake for 40–45 minutes, or until a toothpick comes out mostly clean (no wet batter—some crumbs are okay).

8. Allow to cool completely before removing from the pan. Brownies should be fudgy in the center once cooled.

BANANA CREAM BARS

Makes 9 squares.

Ingredients:

5 tbsp melted butter

Half a box of Nilla Wafers
  (or similar)
  (155.5 g/5.5 oz), plus a dozen
  extra wafers

1 (3 oz) box instant banana
  cream pudding

1 cup (244 g/8.6 oz) whole milk

8 oz (225 g) cream cheese
  (softened)

2 cups (480 g/17 oz)
  heavy whipping cream

2–3 bananas (sliced)

Tip: You can use the
batter of this recipe as
a banana pudding.

Directions:

1. Preheat the oven to 350°F.

2. Crush half the wafers into fine pieces (you can do this by hand or using a food processor).

3. Pour the crushed wafers into a large bowl along with the melted butter. Combine and pour into a greased 8x8" pan.

4. Bake for 8 minutes, then set aside and allow to cool.

5. In a medium bowl, use a hand mixer to beat the cream until whipped. Set aside.

6. In a large bowl, combine the instant pudding mix and milk. Then mix in the softened cream cheese and ½ cup of the whipped cream.

7. Pour the mixture on top of the cooled crust, then top with a layer of sliced bananas.

8. Top with the remaining whipped cream and a few more crushed wafers.

9. Refrigerate for 4 hours or overnight.

10. Slice into 9 squares, then top each with sliced banana, whipped cream, and a whole wafer. Serve immediately (cold).

COOKIE BUTTER COOKIES

Makes 10–12 cookies.

Ingredients:

½ cup (113 g/4 oz) salted butter (softened)

½ cup (125 g/4.4 oz) melted cookie butter

1 egg and 1 egg yolk

1 tsp vanilla extract

½ cup (100 g/3.5 oz) brown sugar

¼ cup (50 g/1.8 oz) granulated sugar

½ cup (80 g/3 oz) white chocolate chips

3 crushed Biscoff cookies (or similar)

1 tsp baking soda

1⅓ cups (173 g/6.1 oz) all-purpose flour

3 Biscoff cookies (or similar), cut in half

Tip: You can also use this recipe to make smaller cookies, or even a cookie skillet.

Directions:

1. Preheat the oven to 350ºF.

2. In a large bowl, combine butter, both sugars, egg and egg yolk, vanilla, and melted cookie butter.

3. Add in the flour and baking soda.

4. Once combined, add the white chocolate chips and crushed cookies.

5. Using an ice cream scoop, lay out 6 large cookies on a baking sheet lined with parchment paper.

6. Bake for 14 minutes and remove from oven. Place half a cookie into the top of each of the cookies.

7. Leave them on the baking sheet for an extra 5 minutes before removing from the pan.

CAKE BATTER BLONDIES

Makes 9 large squares.

Ingredients:

½ cup (80 g/3 oz)
    chopped white chocolate

⅓ cup rainbow sprinkles

1 cup (130 g/4.6 oz)
    all-purpose flour

½ cup (113 g/4 oz) butter

½ cup (100 g/3.5 oz)
    brown sugar

¼ cup (50 g/1.8 oz)
    granulated sugar

½ tsp salt

½ tsp baking powder

1 tsp cake batter flavoring

2 eggs

Tip: If you can't find cake batter flavoring, use ½ tsp vanilla and ½ tsp almond extract.

Directions:

1. Preheat the oven to 350ºF and grease the bottom of an 8x8" or 9x9" glass pan (or line with parchment paper).

2. In a large bowl, microwave the butter until partially melted, then add the sugars and vanilla. Mix to combine.

3. Add in the eggs and mix again.

4. Fold in the flour, baking powder, and salt until combined.

5. Add in the white chocolate and sprinkles.

6. Pour the batter into the prepared pan and bake for 28–30 minutes. Allow to cool completely.

THICK CHOCOLATE CHIP COOKIES

Makes 8 large cookies.

Ingredients:

1 cup (227 g/8 oz) salted butter
   (cold and cubed)
1 cup (200 g/7 oz)
   packed brown sugar
½ cup (100 g/3.5 oz)
   granulated sugar
2 eggs (room temperature)
1½ cups (173 g/6 oz) cake flour
1½ cups (195 g/7 oz)
   all-purpose flour
1 tsp baking soda
1 tsp cornstarch
¼ tsp vanilla
2 cups (320 g/12 oz)
   chocolate chips
1 cup (120 g/4 oz) walnuts

Tip: If you don't want to use all the dough at once, freeze it in 6-oz rounds for another time.

Directions:

1. In a large mixing bowl, using a hand mixer, combine your butter and sugars. Mix for a few minutes until smooth and creamy.

2. Add in your eggs and beat until fluffy.

3. Fold in your dry ingredients using a spatula.

4. Add your chocolate chips and walnuts (if using) and gently mix into the dough. Continue mixing **gently** using your hands. This ensures it's all mixed together well without losing air.

5. Refrigerate the dough for 30 minutes, and set your oven to 410ºF.

6. Separate the dough into large 6-oz rounds and place on a silicone baking mat on a baking tray (we tried parchment too, but preferred the results with the silicone mat).

7. Bake for 15 minutes, then remove from the oven and allow to sit on the tray outside the oven for another 10 minutes.

8. Transfer to a dish, wire rack, etc. Allow to cool for another 5 minutes.

CINNAMON ROLL CUPCAKES

Makes 12 cupcakes.

Cupcake Ingredients:

1½ cups (195 g/7 oz)
 all-purpose flour
1 tsp cinnamon
¾ cup (150 g/5.3 oz)
 granulated sugar
1 tsp baking powder
½ tsp salt
8 tbsp butter (room temperature)
2 eggs
1 tsp vanilla
¾ cup (183 g/6.5 oz)
 cinnamon milk
½ cup (20.5 g/1 oz)
 Cinnamon Toast Crunch cereal
 (or anything similar)

Filling Ingredients:

3 tbsp sugar
4 tbsp cinnamon

Icing Ingredients:

5 cups (600 g/21.5 oz)
 powdered sugar
1¼ cup (281 g/10 oz) butter
 (room temperature)
1 tsp vanilla
3 tbsp cinnamon milk
2 tsp cinnamon

Directions:

1. Preheat the oven to 350ºF and line a cupcake tray with cupcake liners.

2. Add 1 cup milk and ½ cup cinnamon cereal to a cup and allow to soak for 10 minutes. Strain and use ¾ cup for cupcake batter. Reserve the remainder for the icing.

3. In a large bowl, whisk together butter, sugar, vanilla, and eggs.

4. Add in the cinnamon, baking powder, and salt.

5. Fold in the flour and cinnamon milk until fully combined.

6. Add about 2 tbsp of batter to each liner, then top with 1 tsp of the cinnamon sugar filling.

7. Swirl the filling into the batter, then top with another 2–3 tbsp of batter, until the cupcake liners are ¾ full.

8. Bake for 15–18 minutes or until a toothpick comes out clean.

9. Place the cupcakes on a cooling rack to cool.

10. While cooling, use a hand mixer to combine the icing ingredients, and place into a piping bag.

11. Pipe each cupcake with the icing. Sprinkle with any remaining cinnamon sugar filling, and top with extra cereal.

Tip: To easily core the center of cupcakes, use the bottom of a large decorating tip.

STRAWBERRY POKE CAKE

Ingredients:

1 box (432 g/15.25 oz)
   white cake mix

3-oz (85 g) box strawberry gelatin

1 cup (227 g/8 oz) boiling water

½ cup (113.5 g/4 oz)
   ice-cold water

8 oz (226 g) Cool Whip or
   homemade whipped cream

1 cup (125 g/4 oz)
   sliced strawberries

Tip: The longer you allow the cake to refrigerate before topping, the more moist it will become.

Directions:

1. Preheat oven as directed on the cake mix box.

2. Prepare the batter as directed and pour into a 9x9" pan lined with parchment paper.

3. Bake according to box instructions until a toothpick comes out clean, and allow the cake to cool completely. When cool, use a fork to poke multiple holes in the top surface of the cake.

4. In a bowl, combine the gelatin mix with the boiling water until fully dissolved.

5. Add the ice-cold water to the gelatin mixture.

6. Pour the mixture over the cake, being sure to get liquid into the holes formed in the cake.

7. Refrigerate for at least 2 hours (up to overnight).

8. Top with Cool Whip or homemade whipped cream and sliced strawberries before serving.

S'MORES-STUFFED COOKIE SKILLET

Makes one 10-inch cookie skillet

Ingredients:

16 tbsp (2 sticks) salted butter (room temperature)

2½ cups (325 g/11.5 oz) all-purpose flour

¾ cup (150 g/5.3 oz) packed brown sugar

¼ cup (50 g/1.8 oz) granulated sugar

2 tsp vanilla

2 eggs (room temperature)

½ tsp salt

1 tsp baking soda

1 cup (160 g/6 oz) milk chocolate chips

4–5 graham cracker squares broken into pieces

5–6 whole marshmallows (we used the ones stuffed with chocolate)

8 marshmallows cut in half for the border

Tip: If you see the marshmallow border browning too quickly, cover with aluminum foil.

Directions:

1. Preheat the oven to 350ºF and grease a 10-inch oven-safe skillet.

2. In a large bowl, using a hand mixer, combine butter, brown sugar, and granulated sugar until smooth and creamy (at least a few minutes).

3. Add in the eggs and vanilla, then beat again until combined and fluffy.

4. Fold in the flour, salt, and baking soda until well incorporated.

5. Mix in the chocolate chips.

6. Spread half of the dough into the prepared skillet, pressing down to smooth it out.

7. Add the whole marshmallows on top of the dough, along with the broken graham crackers.

8. Spread the remainder of the dough on top as much as you can (it's okay if some of the marshmallows show through the dough).

9. Add the cut marshmallows along the edge to create a border.

10. Bake for 30–35 minutes, depending how set you would like your cookie skillet.

11. Remove from the oven and allow to cool in the skillet for another 10 minutes.

5

BREAKFAST *and* BRUNCH

When it comes to breakfast and brunch, are you Team Sweet or Team Savory? From Air Fryer Stuffed French Toast Sticks to Bacon, Egg, and Cheese Breakfast Sliders, this chapter has a little of each to ensure your next brunch get-together has the best of both worlds!

AIR FRYER STUFFED FRENCH TOAST STICKS

Makes 12 sticks.

Ingredients:

8 slices bread of choice
(the thicker the better)

4 eggs

½ cup (122 g/4.3 oz) whole milk

1–2 tbsp cinnamon/sugar mix

1 tsp vanilla

½ cup (145 g/10 oz) Nutella or
hazelnut spread

Tip: Serve with a
side of maple syrup
for easy dipping.

Directions:

1. Whisk together the eggs, milk, vanilla, and cinnamon/sugar.
    Set aside.

2. Spread Nutella (or hazelnut spread) generously on one slice
    of bread and top with another slice to make a "sandwich."

3. Using a knife, cut into thirds, making 3 sticks per sandwich.

4. Repeat this step with the other slices of bread.

5. Dip each side of a stick into the egg mixture, but don't soak.

6. Place in the air fryer on 350°F for 4 minutes, then flip and
    cook for another 3 minutes.

BREAKFAST RING

Serves 4–6.

Ingredients:

1 (226 g/8 oz) can crescent rolls

4 eggs (scrambled)

4 strips bacon
(cooked and crumbled)

1 egg for egg wash

1 ½ cup (6 oz) shredded cheese
of choice

Tip: You can also make a sweet version of this using your favorite ingredients.

Directions:

1. Preheat the oven to 375ºF.

2. Unroll crescent rolls and place triangles together to form a large star shape.

3. Scramble your eggs as you normally would.

4. Add the cooked, crumbled bacon to the scrambled eggs.

5. Add the eggs and bacon onto the ring of the crescent rolls, then top with cheese.

6. Fold the crescents over and ensure they are sealed with the ring. Brush with egg wash.

7. Bake for 18–20 minutes or until golden.

CHOCOLATE CHIP BANANA BREAD

Makes 1 loaf

Ingredients:

1 ½ cups (195 g/6.9 oz)
   all-purpose flour
8 tbsp butter (softened)
⅔ cup (132 g/4.6 oz)
   granulated sugar
1 tsp vanilla
2 mashed ripe bananas
1 tsp baking soda
¼ tsp salt
1 ¼ cup (200 g/7.5 oz)
   milk chocolate chips

Tip: You can also use chopped chocolate for an even richer banana bread.

Directions:

1. Preheat the oven to 350ºF.

2. Line a loaf pan with parchment paper.

3. In a large bowl, using a hand mixer, combine butter, sugar, eggs, and vanilla until creamy and fluffy.

4. Fold in the mashed banana.

5. Fold in the flour, salt, and baking soda.

6. Once combined, add 1 cup chocolate chips.

7. Pour batter into the prepared pan and top with remaining ¼ cup chocolate chips.

8. Bake for 60 minutes.

9. Allow to cool in the pan for 15 minutes before removing for final cooling/slicing.

BIRTHDAY CAKE ROLLS

Makes 8 rolls

Dough Ingredients:

3½ cups (455 g/16.1 oz)
   all-purpose flour
½ cup (58 g/2.2 oz)
   white cake mix
¼ cup (50 g/1.8 oz)
   granulated sugar
¼ cup (57 g/2 oz) butter
1 cup (244 g/8.6 oz) whole milk
1 beaten egg
1 tsp vanilla
1 (0.4 oz) packet instant yeast
5 tbsp rainbow sprinkles

Filling Ingredients:

⅓ cup (66 g/2.1 oz)
   granulated sugar
¼ cup (57 g/2 oz) butter (softened)
Food coloring of choice (optional)

Icing Ingredients:

¼ cup (57 g/2 oz) salted butter
   (softened)
1½ cups (180 g/6.4 oz)
   powdered sugar
1 tsp vanilla
1 tbsp milk or half and half

Tip: Try not to over-roll your dough. You want the dough to still be able to fluff up during baking.

Directions:

1. In the bowl of a stand mixer, combine the flour, cake mix, and yeast, then set aside.

2. In another bowl, combine butter, sugar, and milk, then microwave for 90 seconds.

3. Attach the stand dough hook and turn to medium speed.

4. Pour the milk mixture into the flour mixture in thirds.

5. Add in your beaten egg, also in thirds.

6. Continue mixing on medium speed until the dough forms and comes off the edges of the stand bowl.

7. Bring the dough together with your hands and cover with plastic wrap for about 10–15 minutes.

8. Preheat your oven to 200°F. In a bowl, add your filling ingredients and mix until well combined.

9. Flour your surface and begin to roll out the dough into a large rectangle about ½ inch thick.

10. Add your sprinkles and roll into the dough. Flip the dough over, add sprinkles, and roll into dough again.

11. Spread your filling onto the dough, leaving about 1 inch from the edges of the rectangle clear to help seal your dough.

12. Horizontally roll the dough. Cut the two corners off and discard.

13. Cut the log into pieces depending on how thick you want them (they will rise). We made 8 very large rolls.

14. Place your rolls in a greased 9x9" pan.

15. Turn the oven off (yes, **off**), cover with aluminum foil, and place the rolls in the oven for 30–40 minutes (this is so they rise more before baking).

16. Remove the pan from the oven and the foil from the pan, then turn the oven on to 350°F. Put the rolls back in and bake uncovered for 35 minutes.

17. Allow to cool 10–15 minutes before icing and decorating.

EVERYTHING BAGEL BREAKFAST POCKET

Makes 3 pockets.

Ingredients:

1 roll of puff pastry

4 large eggs

3–5 slices of bacon
   (cooked and crumbled)

1 ½ cup (6 oz) shredded cheese
   of choice

Everything bagel seasoning

Tip: Don't be afraid to
add a decent amount
of filling—remember,
puff pastry expands
while cooking, and you
want your pockets to be
nice and full.

Directions:

1. Preheat the oven to 350°F.

2. Allow the roll of puff pastry to sit on the counter for 20 minutes, or until soft enough to work with.

3. Cook your bacon as you normally would and set aside.

4. Scramble 3 of the eggs, again as you normally would.

5. Combine the scrambled eggs with the cooked bacon.

6. Cut the roll of puff pastry into 6 equal rectangles.

7. Add a layer of shredded cheese to 3 of the rectangles, then top with the scrambled egg/bacon mixture.

8. Whisk the remaining egg into a small bowl to create an egg wash.

9. Brush the edges of the filled rectangles with egg wash.

10. Top each of the 3 rectangles with the remaining 3 pieces of dough to create 3 "pockets."

11. Using a fork, press down the edges of the dough to seal them together.

12. Poke a few holes in the top of each pocket to create air vents.

13. Brush the tops of the pockets with egg wash and sprinkle with everything bagel seasoning.

14. Bake for 18–20 minutes.

BACON, EGG, *and* CHEESE BREAKFAST SLIDERS

Makes 12 mini sliders

Ingredients:

1 pack Hawaiian rolls

7 large eggs

2 tbsp whole milk

16 oz (453 g) bag shredded
   cheddar cheese

8–10 slices bacon, cooked and
   broken into pieces

1 tsp salt

2 tbsp melted butter

1 tsp garlic powder

1 tbsp dry parsley

Extra parsley for sprinkling

Tip: Add a few sprinkles on top of the buns before baking for some extra cheesy crunch.

Directions:

1. Preheat the oven to 350°F.

2. Combine eggs, milk, and salt. Beat eggs until bubbly/frothy.

3. Scramble the eggs on medium heat until just set and fluffy, but still slightly wet. They will continue to cook later in the oven.

4. Cut the buns across the middle to create a bottom half and top half (don't separate the buns from each other).

5. Place the bottom buns into a greased 9x9" pan and top them with half the cheese, scrambled egg, bacon, remaining half of cheese, and then the top buns.

6. Melt the butter, garlic powder, and parsley. Brush the tops of the buns with the melted garlic butter.

7. Bake 15 minutes (check at 10 minutes; if the tops are browning too quickly, cover with foil for the remaining 5 minutes).

FRUITY CEREAL
BAKED MINI DONUTS

Makes 8 mini donuts.

Donut Ingredients:

1 cup (130 g/4.6 oz)
   all-purpose flour
½ cup (100 g/3.5 oz)
   granulated sugar
1 cup (244 g/8.6 oz) whole milk
¾ cup (25 g/1 oz)
   Fruity Pebbles (or similar) cereal
1 egg
½ tsp salt
1 tsp baking powder
1 tbsp vegetable oil

Icing Ingredients:

1 cup (120 g/4.3 oz)
   powdered sugar
1½–2 tbsp cereal milk
½ tsp vanilla
Couple drops food coloring
   (optional)
Sprinkle of crushed Fruity Pebbles
   (or similar) cereal

Tip: Use the base of this recipe for any flavor cereal donuts you would like.

Directions:

1. Preheat the oven to 350ºF.

2. In a cup, add the milk and ½ cup cereal. Allow to soak for 10 minutes, then strain the cereal out, reserving the milk.

3. In a large bowl, combine flour, sugar, baking powder, salt, vanilla, and egg.

4. Once combined, add ½ cup of the cereal milk and fully mix into the batter.

5. Fold in the remaining ¼ cup of cereal.

6. Add the batter to a piping bag and pipe into donut cavities, filling each ¾ full.

7. Bake for 8–10 minutes.

8. Allow donuts to cool for a few minutes, then remove from pan and allow to cool another 5 minutes.

9. Combine icing ingredients until desired consistency, then dip each donut into the icing.

10. Top with crushed cereal.

PUMPKIN CHEESECAKE MONKEY BREAD

Makes one 10-inch Bundt panful.

Ingredients:

2 (12.4 oz) cans cinnamon rolls

3–4 oz cream cheese (softened)

¾ cup (150 g/5.3 oz) granulated sugar

½ cup (10 g/3.5 oz) brown sugar

½ cup (112.5/4 oz) pumpkin purée

8 tbsp salted butter

Pumpkin spice seasoning

Tip: This recipe also works with regular cinnamon rolls, if you can't find the pumpkin rolls or if they're out of season.

Directions:

1. Preheat the oven to 350ºF.

2. Cut each cinnamon roll slice into quarters.

3. In a large bowl, mix the sugar, brown sugar, and pumpkin spice seasoning, then toss the cinnamon roll pieces in the mixture.

4. Add the coated pieces to a greased Bundt pan.

5. Over medium low heat, combine butter, pumpkin purée, and cream cheese until completely melted.

6. Pour the mixture over the cinnamon roll pieces. Bang the Bundt pan a few times to ensure it's fully coated.

7. Bake for 45 minutes. Allow to cool in the Bundt pan, then flip over onto a plate.

8. Pour the icing that came with the cinnamon rolls over the top.

2off

COOKIE BUTTER CINNAMON ROLLS

Makes 12 rolls.

Dough Ingredients:
4½ cups (585 g/20.7 oz) all-purpose flour
1 tsp salt
2 (0.4 oz) packets instant yeast
1 cup (244 g/8.6 oz) milk
½ cup (113g/4 oz) butter
¼ cup (50g/1.8 oz) granulated sugar
2 eggs

Filling Ingredients:
1 cup (200 g/7 oz) brown sugar
4 tbsp cinnamon
¼ cup (57 g/2 oz) butter (softened)
¼ cup (62.5 g/2.2 oz) melted cookie butter

Frosting Ingredients:
1½ cups (180 g/6.4 oz) powdered sugar
5–6 tbsp heavy cream
2 tbsp melted butter
1 tsp vanilla
3 tbsp melted cookie butter
4–6 crushed Biscoff cookies

Tip: Try adding ¼ cup warm heavy cream over the cinnamon rolls in the pan before baking for an even softer texture.

Directions:

1. In a stand mixer using a dough hook, add the flour, salt, and yeast. In a small microwave-safe bowl, combine ½ cup butter, ¼ cup sugar, and 1 cup milk. Heat in microwave for 60 seconds.

2. Start the mixer on low speed and slowly add the warm milk mixture.

3. Change the mixer to medium speed and add one egg at a time.

4. Once a dough begins to form, turn the mixer back to low speed.

5. Continue mixing dough until it forms a ball.

6. Remove the dough and continue to knead over a lightly floured surface. If the dough is too sticky, add 1 tbsp flour at a time until it is no longer sticky.

7. Spread olive oil along the edge of a bowl and place the dough in the bowl. Cover with a damp kitchen towel for 30 minutes.

8. Roll the dough out into a large rectangle (ours was about 13x18").

9. In a small bowl, combine brown sugar and cinnamon. In another small bowl, soften ¼ cup butter until spreadable (do not completely melt it).

10. Brush the butter onto the rectangle, leaving ¼–½ inch along the edges free of butter.

11. Spread the cinnamon sugar mixture all over the buttered area and pat down.

12. Roll the rectangle up tightly and cut off excess at edges.

5: Breakfast and Brunch

13. Cut into 12 equal pieces and place in a greased glass pan.

14. At this time, preheat your oven to 175ºF and then turn the oven **off**. Do not skip this step.

15. Place the pan into the preheated oven with the oven **turned off**.

16. Allow to proof a second time for 20–30 minutes.

17. After 20–30 minutes, turn your oven back on to 350ºF while the rolls are inside.

18. Bake for 25 minutes or until just golden, then let cool for 10–15 minutes.

19. In a medium bowl, combine powdered sugar, melted butter, vanilla, and heavy cream until a glaze forms. If it's too thick, microwave in 10-second bursts until desired consistency.

20. Pour glaze over the cinnamon rolls and melt down about 3 tbsp cookie butter, then drizzle over the top of the glazed cinnamon rolls. Sprinkle with crushed Biscoff cookies.

6

TWO-TO-SEVEN-INGREDIENT RECIPES

We're living in an era when sometimes less is smore. The recipes in this chapter contain minimal ingredients that are easily accessible for all to enjoy. From viral two-ingredient recipes to trendy seven-ingredient pastry braids, this chapter can meet all your snacking needs!

AIR FRYER STRAWBERRY BREAKFAST TARTS

Makes 3 Breakfast Tarts.

Tart Ingredients:

1 roll of refrigerated pie crust
Strawberry jam (or any other jam)

Topping Ingredients:

1 cup (120 g/4.3 oz)
   powdered sugar
1–2 tbsp milk or half and
   half Sprinkles
Food coloring (optional)

Tip: Try it with
blueberry jam, too.

Directions:

1. Roll out your pie crust and cut into 6 squares.

2. Add your filling to the center of one square and gently spread it out, leaving the edges clear.

3. Top with another square of crust and use a fork to seal the edges. Repeat for the other squares.

4. Poke some holes into the tops and air fry for 10 minutes at 350°F (we recommend flipping halfway).

5. Allow to cool slightly, then top with your icing/sprinkles.

S'MORES PASTRY BRAID

Makes 1 braid.

Ingredients:

1 puff pastry dough sheet

1 6 oz chocolate bar

3 large scoops of Nutella or
 hazelnut spread

1 whisked egg for egg wash

½ cup (27.5 g/1 oz)
 mini marshmallows

2 sheets of graham cracker
 (one broken, one crushed)

Chocolate chips for topping

Tip: You can make
many variations of
this recipe, including
savory braids.

Directions:

1. Preheat the oven to 350ºF.

2. Using a slightly thawed pastry sheet, add the chocolate bar, hazelnut spread, the broken graham cracker pieces, and marshmallows to the center.

3. Using a knife or pizza cutter, make 1-inch cuts diagonally along the sides of the dough.

4. Remove the corners and fold the top flat over the filling first. Then begin to braid the dough down. Before braiding the bottom pieces, fold the bottom flap up above the filling.

5. Brush with an egg wash, adding the crushed graham cracker and some chocolate chips.

6. Bake for 25 minutes and allow to cool slightly.

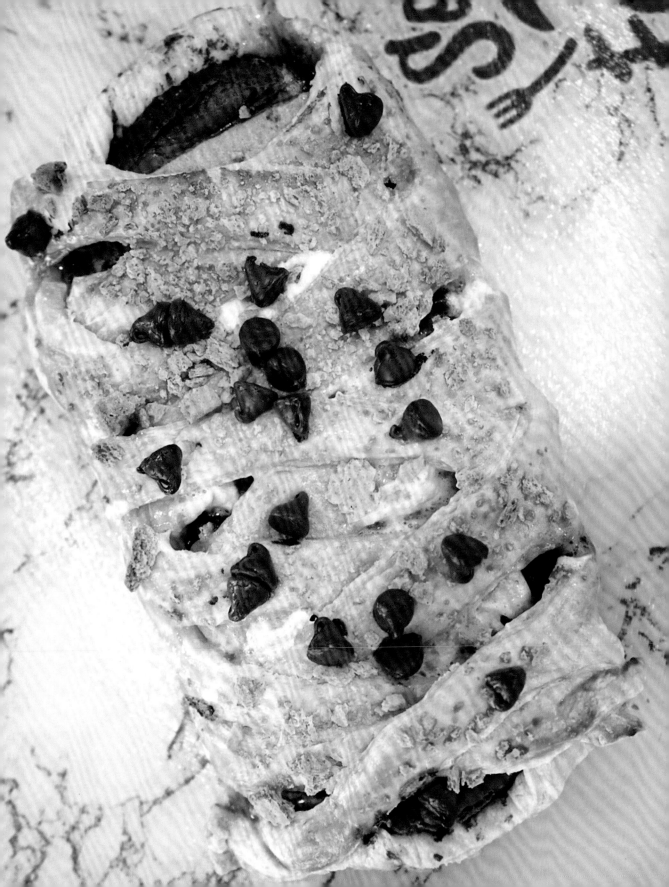

TWO-INGREDIENT BAGELS

Makes 4 bagels.

Ingredients:

1 cup (285 g/10 oz) Greek yogurt

1½ cups (190 g/6.6 oz)
  self-rising flour

Egg wash

Everything bagel seasoning
  (optional)

Tip: This dough works as a pizza base as well.

Directions:

1. In a large bowl, combine one cup of the flour with the Greek yogurt. Mix until it just starts to come together.

2. Pour the mixture onto a lightly floured flat surface and knead with your hands until it fully comes together, adding the remaining flour as you are kneading.

3. Once a smooth ball forms, cut into 4 equal pieces.

4. Roll each piece out individually, then create circles by joining the ends together to create a bagel shape.

5. Place on a tray lined with parchment paper.

6. Lightly brush the top of each bagel with egg wash and sprinkle everything bagel seasoning on top (optional).

7. Bake at 350°F for 20 minutes (until golden brown), then turn the heat to broil and cook another 5 minutes. Watch carefully to not burn the bagels during broiling.

BIRTHDAY CAKE CRISPY TREATS

Makes 9 squares.

Ingredients:

6 tbsp salted butter

10 oz (283 g) mini marshmallows

6 cups (180 g/6 oz) Rice Krispies
(or similar) cereal

½ cup (58 g/2.2 oz) cake mix
(any kind works)

4 oz melted white chocolate
for drizzle

5 tbsp cup rainbow sprinkles

Directions:

1. Over medium heat, melt the butter, then add the marshmallows.

2. Once fully melted, remove from heat and mix in the cereal, cake mix, and sprinkles.

3. Pour the mixture into an 8x8" or 9x9" greased or parchment-lined pan, pressing down slightly.

4. Allow to cool for 30 minutes before slicing.

5. Drizzle with melted white chocolate and extra sprinkles.

Tip: If you don't want the sprinkles to bleed into the treats, just add them at the end with the white chocolate drizzle, but we personally think it gives the treats a fun color.

GARLIC CHEESE BOMBS

Makes 8 cheese bombs.

Ingredients:

1 16.3 oz (462 g) can
refrigerated biscuit dough

4–6 ounces fresh mozzarella
cheese (cubed)

3 tbsp butter

1 tsp garlic powder

1 tsp Italian seasoning

Sprinkle of dry parsley

Pinch of salt

Tip: Serve with pizza
or marinara sauce.

Directions:

1. Preheat the oven to 400°F and line a baking sheet with parchment paper.

2. Place each biscuit on the prepared pan, pressing down slightly to flatten a bit. Top each biscuit with a piece of cubed cheese.

3. Wrap each biscuit around the cheese to create balls. Make sure to tightly seal the edges so there are no escape holes.

4. Place each ball on the prepared pan with the seal side down and bake for 12 minutes or until golden brown.

5. While the biscuits are baking, melt the butter, garlic powder, Italian seasoning, and salt in the microwave.

6. Brush each of the biscuits with the melted butter mixture and sprinkle with dry parsley.

TWO-INGREDIENT CHOCOLATE SOUFFLÉ

Serves 2.

Ingredients:

½ cup (145 g/10 oz) Nutella or
   hazelnut spread

2 eggs

Powdered sugar (optional)

Tip: Serve immediately after adding the powdered sugar to avoid deflation.

Directions:

1. Preheat the oven to 375°F.

2. Separate the egg yolks from the whites and place them in separate medium-sized bowls.

3. Add the hazelnut spread to the bowl with the yolks. Beat using a hand mixer until it comes together, then set aside.

4. Using a clean and dry hand mixer, beat the egg whites until stiff peaks form.

5. Fold half of the egg white mixture into the egg yolk/hazelnut spread mixture.

6. Repeat with the remaining egg whites.

7. Pour into 2 greased ramekins and bake for 17–18 minutes.

8. Allow to cool for a couple of minutes, then sprinkle them with powdered sugar (optional).

HAM *and* CHEESE PINWHEELS

Serves 2.

Ingredients:

1 sheet puff pastry

9 slices of ham

1 ½ cups (6 oz) shredded
   cheddar cheese

3 tbsp ranch dressing

Tip: Drizzle the tops
with some buffalo
sauce after baking.

Directions:

1. Allow the puff pastry sheet to come to almost room temperature, where it is easy to work with.

2. Spread the ranch dressing onto the sheet.

3. Top with ham and cheese.

4. Roll the sheet up lengthwise into a tight log and place in the fridge for 30 minutes.

5. Preheat oven to 375ºF.

6. Slice the ends of the log to make it even, and then use a serrated knife to cut half-inch-thick slices.

7. Place on a baking sheet and bake for 18 minutes.

TWO-INGREDIENT HAZELNUT TWIST

Serves 2.

Ingredients:

1 sheet puff pastry
½ cup (145 g/10 oz) Nutella or
    hazelnut spread
Egg wash (optional)
Sea salt (optional)

Tip: Add some fresh
fruit during step 2.

Directions:

1. Allow the puff pastry sheet to come to near room temperature, where it is easy to work with.

2. Spread the Nutella (or hazelnut spread) over the center of the sheet.

3. Roll the sheet up lengthwise into a tight log and place in the fridge for 20 minutes.

4. Preheat oven to 350°F.

5. Cut down the center of the roll lengthwise so you have 2 pieces.

6. Begin to twist the 2 pieces together to create one larger twist.

7. Place on a baking sheet and top with egg wash (optional).

8. Bake for 30–35 minutes, or until golden and cooked through.

9. Sprinkle the top with sea salt (optional).

ABOUT THE AUTHORS

Shalean and Stephanie Ghitis are the owners of @soflofooodie, a fully licensed food and beverage blog that launched in 2016. SoFloFooodie focuses on content creation primarily in the recipe space and has amassed over 3.5 million followers across platforms. Shay and Steph have become known for their viral recipe content and have been featured on several media outlets, such as NBC6 News for their viral Unicorn Rainbow Cheesecake, *Good Morning America*, TikTok Newsroom as a top 10 TikTok creator in the food category for 2020, *Insider*, Food Network, and more. Notable partnerships include Pillsbury, Funfetti, DoorDash, Dunkin', Nestlé, Uber Eats, Ninja Kitchen, Sabra, McDonald's, and more.

When not developing recipes or creating content, Shay and Steph work full-time jobs on the administration team at a school for individuals on the autism spectrum. Autism spectrum disorder (ASD) has become a major part of their lives, which is part of their drive to create easy and accessible recipes using everyday ingredients that individuals of all ages and abilities can enjoy.

INDEX

Mango Publishing, established in 2014, publishes an eclectic list of books by diverse authors—both new and established voices—on topics ranging from business, personal growth, women's empowerment, LGBTQ studies, health, and spirituality to history, popular culture, time management, decluttering, lifestyle, mental wellness, aging, and sustainable living. We were recently named 2019 *and* 2020's #1 fastest-growing independent publisher by *Publishers Weekly*. Our success is driven by our main goal, which is to publish high-quality books that will entertain readers as well as make a positive difference in their lives.

Our readers are our most important resource; we value your input, suggestions, and ideas. We'd love to hear from you—after all, we are publishing books for you!

Please stay in touch with us and follow us at:

Facebook: Mango Publishing
Twitter: @MangoPublishing
Instagram: @MangoPublishing
LinkedIn: Mango Publishing
Pinterest: Mango Publishing
Newsletter: mangopublishinggroup.com/newsletter

Join us on Mango's journey to reinvent publishing, one book at a time.